Discus Dynamo

Phil Kettle
illustrated by Craig Smith

Distributed in
the United States of America
by Pacific Learning
P.O. Box 2723
Huntington Beach, CA
92647-0723

Website:
www.pacificlearning.com

Published by Black Hills
(an imprint of Toocool Rules
Pty Ltd)
PO Box 2073
Fitzroy MDC VIC 3065
Australia
61+3+9419-9406

First published in the United States by Black Hills in 2004.
American editorial by Pacific Learning in 2004.
Text copyright © Phillip Kettle, 2003.
Illustration copyright © Toocool Rules Pty Limited, 2003.

 a black dog and Springhill book

Printed in China through Colorcraft Ltd, Hong Kong

ISBN 1 920924 19 1
PL-6219

10 9 8 7 6 5 4 3 2 1   08 07 06 05 04

Contents

Toocool's mom

Mr. Lopez

Scott

Dog

Toocool

Bert

Chapter 1
Olympic Athlete

It can take some people years of hard training to throw a discus really well. It took me no time at all. One morning I threw a Frisbee at school. Everyone cheered and clapped.

The Frisbee flew into the air and disappeared into the clouds. At lunchtime, it finally landed—right in the middle of Scott's spaghetti surprise.

If I were that good with a Frisbee, imagine how good I would be with a discus!

The next morning, I decided I was going to compete in the discus event at the Olympic Games.

An Olympic athlete isn't an ordinary person. You have to follow special routines. You have to eat special food.

"Toocool, if you don't get out here this minute I'll feed your breakfast to Dog," yelled the coach.

An athlete also has to listen to the coach.

After breakfast, I made my bed and cleaned my bedroom. This was a special training exercise the coach had invented. It helped warm up my muscles.

I looked in the mirror. I was looking good. Soon, millions of people would see me on television. I'd be standing with a gold medal around my neck. I'd be singing the national anthem. I just needed to learn all the words.

Chapter 2
The Parade of Athletes

My training partner arrived before the coach could give me another special exercise.

"What are we doing today?" asked Scott.

"Today we're trying out for the discus event. Whoever wins will be on the U.S. Track and Field team. I can't wait to get there. Maybe you could be an alternate."

"I'm much better than you at discus throwing," said Scott.

"You might think you're better than I am, but I know I'm the greatest discus thrower the world has ever seen."

"You think you're good at everything," said Scott.

I had to agree. I was good at everything, especially sports.

"First we should practice for the Opening Ceremony parade of athletes," I said.

We grabbed our flags.

"Ready?" I asked.

"Let's go," said Scott.

Scott and I marched past the athletes' dormitories and into the stadium. A crowd had gathered to watch us. Their cheers were deafening.

We waved our American flags as we marched around the arena. Then an announcement came over the loudspeaker. It was the stadium manager.

"Toocool, what have you done with my sheets? Are those my broom handles?"

It was time to let the Olympic Games begin.

Chapter 3
Discus Trials

The throwing ring had already been marked out.

"Okay," I said. "We'll do three throws each. The winner will go on to the Olympics."

"Maybe we should practice first," said Scott.

"You can practice if you need to," I said.

"I don't need practice to beat you, Toocool," said Scott.

We warmed up. I did a few stretches. I flexed my huge shoulder muscles.

Scott stretched his not-so-big shoulder muscles. He threw a lemon for practice. There was a loud bang as the lemon landed on top of the garage roof.

"Maybe you should keep practicing," I said.

Winning was going to be too easy.

The siren rang for the trial to start. I was only a few throws away from going to the Olympics.

The crowd stood up and cheered as we approached the ring. The roar sounded like thunder.

"The longest throw wins," I said. "You go first."

"Says who?" said Scott.

"Says the person who owns the stadium," I said.

Scott stepped into the ring. He picked up the discus and held it in one hand. He stood toward the back of the ring.

He swung the discus in a half-circle around his body. Then he started to spin around crazily.

"Hurry up," I said.

Scott threw the discus with all his strength. It looked good in the air. Then it landed on the stadium roof.

"Foul," I said.

Chapter 4

Discus Disaster

Winning this competition was only a few minutes away.

"Two throws left," I said.

"You better get the discus off the roof," said Scott.

"Why should I? You threw it there," I said.

"You wrecked my concentration," said Scott.

Just then, the discus slid
down the roof. It landed right
on Scott's head. He looked like
a mushroom.

Scott's second throw landed
in the judges' box. His last
throw looked good as it flew
high and long. Then Dog
leaped up and grabbed it from
mid-air.

"That was my best throw,"
Scott complained.

It was my turn. I dusted my hands with chalk. This would keep the discus from slipping.

I stood in the back of the ring. In a graceful whirl, I spun around the perfect one-and-a-half times. Then I let go of the discus.

At that moment, a freak gust of wind swept through the stadium. The discus wobbled through the air straight into the stadium crowd.

Scott was laughing so hard he couldn't stand up.

"What do you call that?" he asked.

I ignored him. He was just trying to ruin my focus. I'd show him.

Dog rescued the discus from the crowd. Then he took it right to the judges' box.

"I win, I win, I win," sang Scott.

It took a while to get the discus back from Dog. That had been a practice throw. Now I really meant it.

In the middle of my second throw, Scott began singing.

"I am the best. Forget the rest," he sang.

The discus left my hand too early. This time it went backward. It bounced off the scoreboard and scared an official out of his seat.

Chapter 5
Winning Throw

Scott was still laughing. I ignored him.

It was my last throw. Instead of throwing too hard, I relaxed my body. I took a deep breath. I whirled around in a tight spin.

The discus left my hand. It spun high and steady. It spun right out of the stadium. It was a winner.

"Foul," said Scott. "Your foot went outside the ring."

He was just jealous.

I grabbed a flag. I ran around the arena waving it at the crowd.

"Toocool, Toocool, Toocool," they chanted.

Then there was a cheer from outside the stadium. It was Mr. Lopez. He was always the first to congratulate me.

"Toocool, what have you done to my tomato plants?"

It felt good to be an Olympic athlete. Winning a gold medal for discus would be easy, but the Olympics were a long way off.

To stay in competition shape, I'd need to keep busy with other sports. I wonder what sport I should try next...
The End!

Toocool's
Discus Glossary

Ceremony—Actions performed on an important occasion.

Dormitories—The rooms where the athletes stay during the Olympic Games.

Judge—Someone who gives a decision or opinion on the winner of a contest or competition.

Routine—Something that is done in the same way or at the same time or place.

Stadium—A large sports arena with seats for spectators.

Toocool's Map
The Track and Field Stadium

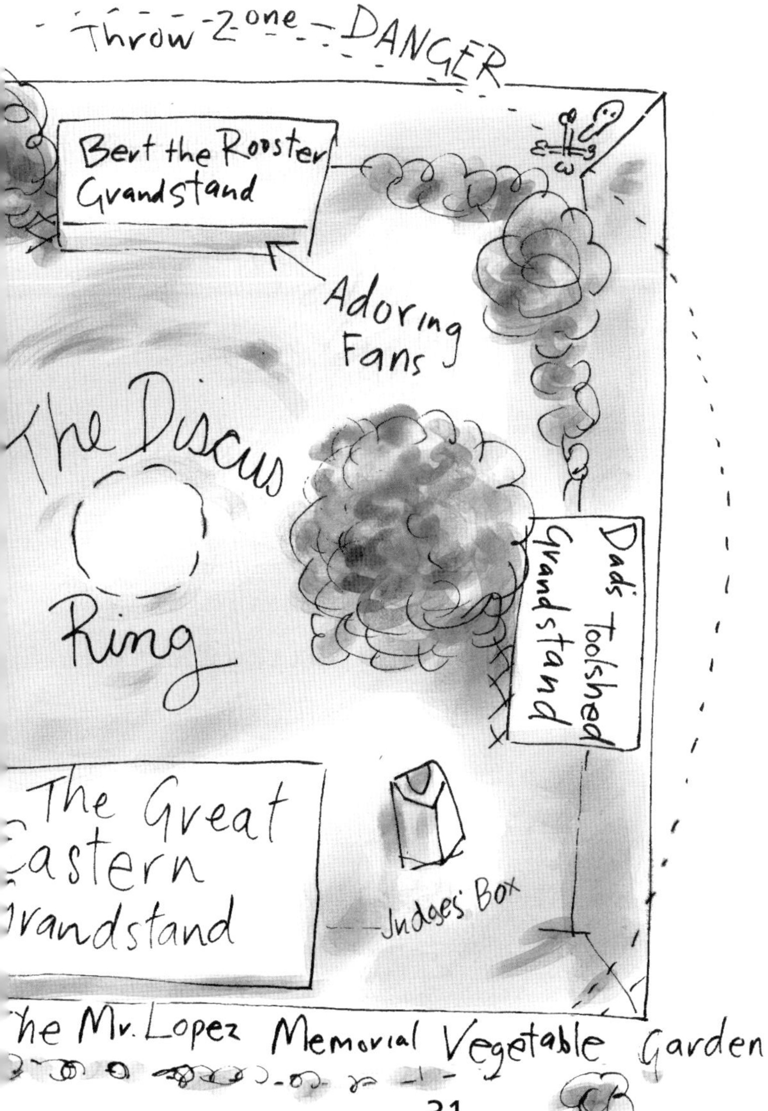

Throw-zone—DANGER

Bert the Rooster Grandstand

Adoring Fans

The Discus

Ring

Dad's Toolshed Grandstand

The Great Eastern Grandstand

Judges' Box

The Mr. Lopez Memorial Vegetable Garden

31

Toocool's Quick Summary
The Discus

The discus has been around for a long time. People in ancient Greece really enjoyed this sport. In fact, it was one of their favorites.

In those days, the discus was made of either bronze, stone, lead, or iron. The discus had a different size and shape depending on the age of the contestant and exactly what competition it was being thrown in.

Before the throw, the contestants would rub their hands and the discus with sand. This helped to keep the discus from slipping. Today we use a special kind of chalk instead of sand.

Sometimes in a contest you might get a few warm-up throws. Don't try to throw the discus as far as you can. Save your energy for the throws that count.

Discus competitors get either three or six competition throws, depending on how many people are competing. Then their longest throw is counted. You don't have to be strong to throw the discus really far. The trick is to be relaxed when you throw. You can never be too cool!

The **Discus** and the Frisbee

The Discus

1. Hold like this. 2. Spin one-and-a-half times. 3. Throw.

My Frisbee

Hold like this. 2. Throw.
. Watch Frisbee fly along ground,
or in other direction.

Q & A with Toocool
He Answers His Own Questions

 **What makes you so good at throwing a discus?**

I think it helps that I'm a total champion at all sports that I play. You have to be in great shape.

How did you get interested in discus throwing?

The first time I threw a Frisbee, I was a natural. Instantly, I was the best Frisbee player in school. From there I went to the discus.

What's the difference between throwing a discus and throwing a Frisbee?

A major difference is that Frisbees are meant to be caught. Dog is the greatest catcher that I've ever seen. Of course, Dog learned from watching me. Frisbees are lighter, too. You use your hand, arm, and the strength of your shoulders to throw a discus. You only use your fingers and wrist to flick a Frisbee.

 Where do you train?

I do my discus training at school, sometimes at lunchtime and sometimes after school has finished. A lot of kids stop what they're doing just to watch me in action. I do look good.

37

Is there anywhere you can't train?

I don't throw my discus in the house anymore. The discus seems to knock things over—even when I'm being really careful. I'm still paying for a vase that got knocked off the coffee table. (It was a very good throw.) I also don't train near the chicken coop, ever since Mom yelled at me. Was it my fault that the chickens squawked so noisily as they were cheering for me?

Do you need to own a discus to practice throwing one?

Sometimes Dog hides my discus, and I need to find something else to throw. I've used paint-can lids, and even plastic plates.

Throwing the discus was a sport in ancient Greece. Could you ever see yourself as an ancient Greek athlete?

An athlete is an athlete, and I am a good one. I don't think it matters where you are in history. I would be a great ancient Greek athlete, although I prefer my football uniform to those sheets they wore back then. Also, Mom wouldn't be happy if I wore her sheets while I competed in my favorite sports. She still hasn't gotten over us using her sheets for flags.

Discus Quiz
How Much Do You
Know about the Discus?

Q1 Should you use a plate from the kitchen as a discus?
A. Only if you don't have a discus. *B.* Only if you want to get into trouble with your mom.
C. No, they don't bounce.

Q2 What should you do if your dog runs away with your discus?
A. Chase the dog until he drops it. *B.* Find another discus. *C.* Go home and sulk.

Q3 What happens when you throw a discus against the wind?
A. It doesn't go as far as it could.
B. It flies away. **C.** It goes faster.

Q4 What should you do if your discus gets stuck in a tree?
A. Wait for wind. **B.** Let Scott get it. **C.** Hope a squirrel drops it.

Q5 Should you throw your discus in the house?
A. Yes, if you want to get into trouble. **B.** No, there's no room.
C. No. Vases cost too much.

Q6 Are you supposed to catch a discus?
A. If you can. **B.** No. **C.** Only if Scott throws it.

Q7 How far do you think you can throw a discus?
A. 100 yards. *B.* Farther than Toocool. *C.* Not as far as Toocool.

Q8 What did the ancient Greek athletes use on their hands before throwing a discus?
A. Oil. *B.* Mud. *C.* Sand.

Q9 Who do you think would be the best discus thrower?
A. Marcy. *B.* Toocool. *C.* Mr. Lopez.

Q10 What should you use to throw a discus?
A. Your feet. *B.* Just your fingers.
C. Your hand, arm, and shoulders.

ANSWERS

1 C. 2 B. 3 A.

4 B. 5 B. 6 B.

7 C. 8 C. 9 B.

10 C.

If you got ten questions right, you could try out for your school's discus team. If you got more than five right, you could practice in your backyard with Toocool. If you got fewer than five right, you should practice with a round chair cushion so you don't hurt yourself—or anyone else.

Have you read all of
Toocool's adventures?
Don't miss any of his
triumphant wins!

Titles in the Toocool series